10 Days of English Cursive Handwriting Workbook

영어 필기체 10일 완성 노트

GBB

10일 만에 영어 필기체를 쓰고 읽을 수 있는, 친절한 영어 필기체 가이드

시대물이든 현대물이든 미국이나 영국 영화에 자주 나오는 장면이 있어요. 등장인물이 탁자에 앉아 잉크에 적신 깃펜이나 만년필로 빛바랜 종이에 필기체를 멋지게 써내려가는 모습이지요. 아름다운 글자체와 우아한 손놀림을 보고 있자면 필기체를 쓰는 것만으로도 지친 일상을 벗어나 마음의 여유를 만끽할 수 있을 것 같아요.

누군가가 필기체로 장식된 카드를 받고 기뻐하는 모습, 다이어리에 필기체로 하루 일을 적으며 힐링하는 모습을 상상한다면 당장이라도 필기체 연습을 시작하고 싶어질지 몰라요. 학교에서 영어 필기체를 배우지는 않지만, 필기체는 우리 주변에서 널리 쓰이고 있어요. 외국에서 생활했거나 해외 출장 경험이 있다면, 얼마나 영어 필기체가 다양하게 쓰이고 꼭 필요한지 잘 알 거예요. 게다가 손으로 직접 글씨를 쓰면 두뇌에 자극을 주기 때문에 생활을 훨씬 의욕적이고 창의적으로 바꿔준답니다.

《영어 필기체 10일 완성 노트》는 가장 기초적인 것부터 시작하기 때문에 필기체를 써본 적이 전혀 없더라도 바로 할 수 있어요. 책을 따라 10일 동안 꾸준히 연습하면 영어 일기와 편지는 물론, 누구도 모방할 수 없는 나만의 '시그니처 서체'까지 만들 수 있답니다.

실용적이고 우아한 취미생활까지 겸할 수 있는 영어 필기체를 익히고 싶다면 이 책으로 시작해보세요!

Contents

들어가는 말

이 책의 구성

이 책의 활용법

필기체 대문자 · 소문자 한눈에 보기

DAY 1   알파벳 Aa부터 Nn까지 연습하는 날   13   ☐

DAY 2   알파벳 Oo부터 Zz까지 연습하는 날   29   ☐

DAY 3   Aa부터 Mm까지 다양한 단어를 연습하는 날   45   ☐

DAY 4   Nn부터 Zz까지 다양한 단어를 연습하는 날   61   ☐

DAY 5   주제별 단어를 연습하는 날   77   ☐
숫자, 월, 요일, 그리스 신, 태양계, 식물

DAY 6   일상에 유용한 단어를 연습하는 날   93   ☐
한국인 성, 유명인 이름, 수도와 나라

DAY 7   문장에 자주 활용되는 단어를 연습하는 날   109   ☐

DAY 8   일상에 유용한 문장을 연습하는 날   121   ☐
일상, 응원·위로의 말, 긍정 확언, 명언

DAY 9   특별한 날에 사용되는 문구를 연습하는 날   133   ☐
크리스마스, 새해, 생일, 기념의 말

DAY 10   세계 문학 작품의 제목과 문단을 연습하는 날   145   ☐
오만과 편견, 노인과 바다, 어린 왕자

Final Day   영어 필기체 마스터 수료증   160   ☐

차근차근, 탄탄하게
10일 만에 마스터하는 나의 영어 필기체

☆ Step by Step!

알파벳부터 짧은 단어, 긴 단어, 문장, 문단 순으로 차근차근, 다양하게 연습하면서 영어 필기체의 기본기를 탄탄하게 쌓을 수 있어요.

Day 1 ~ Day 2   A부터 Z까지 대문자와 소문자 알파벳을 연습할 수 있어요.

Day 3 ~ Day 4   A부터 Z까지 짧은 단어와 긴 단어를 연습하면서
                 이어 쓰기를 익힐 수 있어요.

Day 5 ~ Day 7   일상에서 자주 쓰는 주제별 단어를 연습할 수 있어요.

Day 8 ~ Day 9   알아두면 쓸모 있는 문구들을 연습할 수 있어요.

Day10   세계 문학 작품의 제목과 문장, 문단을 연습하면서
                 영어 필기체를 완성할 수 있어요.

☆ 지루하지 않게, 재미있게 익히는 단어들

한국인의 성씨, 그리스 신화의 12신, 태양계, 우리 주변의 식물 이름처럼 자주 입에 오르내리는 영어 단어들을 필기체로 써볼 수 있어요. 닮고 싶은 유명인들의 이름, 세계의 국가

와 수도 이름 등을 써보며 재미있게 영어 필기체를 연습할 수 있어요.

☆ 알아두면 유익한 테마별 문구들
긍정 확언, 특별한 기념일에 사용되는 표현을 영어 필기체로 익혀서 나와 친구, 가족들에게 손글씨로 응원과 사랑을 전할 수 있어요.

☆ 세계 문학 작품 속 명문장 수록
세계 문학 작품만큼 영어 필기체와 잘 어울리는 장르는 없을 거예요. 《오만과 편견》, 《노인과 바다》, 《어린 왕자》처럼 감성이 묻어나는 20세기 문학 작품 속 명문장을 영어 필기체로 써보면서 우아한 영어 필기체를 완성할 수 있어요.

☆ 연습하기 전과 후를 확인할 수 있는 연습 공간
자유롭게 연습할 수 있는 연습 페이지(Practice Note)를 넉넉하게 마련했어요. 알파벳, 단어, 문구나 문장을 영어 필기체로 연습한 후 자신만의 필기체로 자유롭게 써보세요. 필기체 연습을 통해 달라진 손글씨의 변화를 확인할 수 있어요.

☆ 10일 후 완성하는 수료증
이 책 마지막에는 수료증이 있어요. 그동안 쌓은 영어 필기체로 수료증을 작성해 완주한 자신을 축하해보세요. 앞으로 더 멋진 영어 필기체 실력을 키우겠다고 다짐하면서 더 큰 목표에 도전해보세요.

취미와 학습을 동시에,
재미있으면서 유용한 영어 필기체

☆ 글씨 교정과 캘리그라피 연습

예쁘고 다양한 필기구를 손에 쥐고 끄적끄적 글씨 쓰는 걸 좋아하는 분들이라면 분명 영어 필기체에 관심이 많을 거예요.

필기체는 참 근사해요. 한 자씩 분리된 정자체와는 맛이 달라요. 알파벳끼리 자연스럽게 이어지기 때문에 아름답거든요. 영어 필기체를 쓸 때는 조화와 균형감이 느껴지도록 손목의 힘, 종이와 펜과의 압을 고려해서 써야 해요.

이 책은 연습 노트이니 편안하게 종이와 펜, 손목의 움직임과 마음을 연결해 천천히 써보세요. 그러면서 자신만의 영문 서체를 창조해보세요. 영어 필기체를 연습하다 보면 글씨체를 교정할 수 있고, 고급스럽고 우아한 영문 캘리그라피에도 도전할 수 있어요.

☆ 쉽고 효과적인 영어 공부

외국 여행, 유학 중에 현지인의 필기체를 해독할 수 없어서 난감한 적이 있을 거예요. 물론 상대방의 글씨체가 악필일 수 있어요. 하지만 영어 필기체의 기본기를 습득한다면 휘갈겨 쓴 영어 필기체도 쉽게 읽을 수 있어요.

영어 필기체를 익히면 문장을 빠르게 쓸 수 있기 때문에 영어 필사나 영단어 공부, 영작할 때 시간을 줄이면서 즐겁게 공부할 수 있어요.

유학생, 외국계 회사에 다니는 분, 외국 생활을 준비하는 분에게 영어 필기체는 선택이 아닌 필수적인 도구예요.

☆ 다양한 필기구로 써보는 시간

연필부터 볼펜, 수성펜, 색연필, 만년필(펜촉의 표면적이 넓은 만년필은 번짐이 생길 수도 있어요)에 이르기까지 다양한 필기구로 영어 필기체를 연습해보세요. 필기구에 따라 잉크의 번짐을 관찰하고 필기체의 곡선, 다른 알파벳과 이어지는 느낌을 체험하면서 자신에게 맞는 필기구를 찾아보세요.

☆ 손글씨를 통한 힐링의 시간

하루하루 좋은 에너지와 풍성한 경험을 얻고 싶은 분들은 다양한 루틴을 만들어 실천해요. 그중의 하나가 손글씨예요. 손글씨는 종이에 자신의 마음을 담아 글을 쓰는 일이지만 공간과 시간, 나의 마음이 하나가 되는 소중한 시간이기도 해요. 영어 필기체 쓰기로 모닝 루틴을 한다면 차분히 마음을 모으면서 힐링의 시간을 가질 수 있어요.

❖일러두기❖
- 영어 필기체는 인쇄된 서체에 따라, 쓰는 방법에 차이가 있을 수 있습니다.
- 특별한 날에 사용되는 문구 중 어버이날은 우리나라 상황에 맞게 만들었습니다.
- 지명의 경우, 영어식 표기를 따랐습니다.

Capital Letters

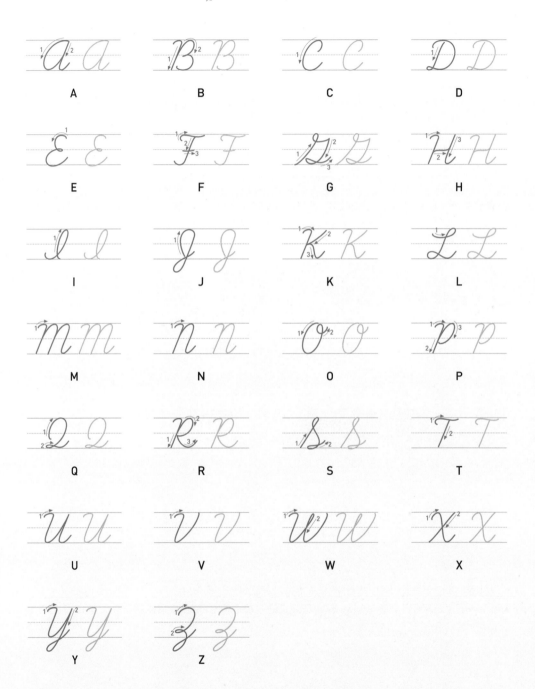

A	B	C	D
E	F	G	H
I	J	K	L
M	N	O	P
Q	R	S	T
U	V	W	X
Y	Z		

Small Letters

•필기체 소문자•

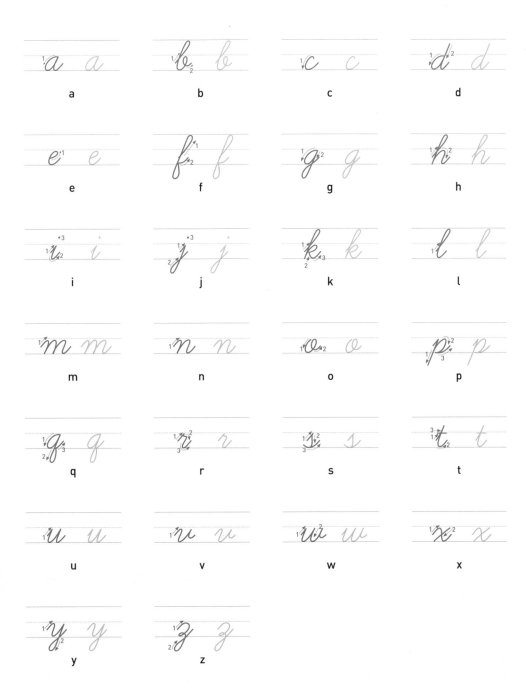

a

b

c

d

e

f

g

h

i

j

k

l

m

n

o

p

q

r

s

t

u

v

w

x

y

z

DAY 1

알파벳 Aa부터 Nn까지
연습하는 날

알파벳 A와 a를 써보세요.

A　**a**

a a a

a a a

a a

a a

a a

a a

모음과 이어 써보세요.

Aa Aa Aa　　　　*aa aa aa*

Ae Ae Ae　　　　*ae ae ae*

Ai Ai Ai　　　　*ai ai ai*

Ao Ao Ao　　　　*ao ao ao*

Au Au Au　　　　*au au au*

알파벳 B와 b를 써보세요.

B B B

b b b

B B

b b

B B

b b

모음과 이어 써보세요.

Ba Ba Ba   ba ba ba

Be Be Be   be be be

Bi Bi Bi   bi bi bi

Bo Bo Bo   bo bo bo

Bu Bu Bu   bu bu bu

Alphabet - Cc

알파벳 C와 c를 써보세요.

C C C

c c c

C C

c c

C C

c c

모음과 이어 써보세요.

Ca Ca Ca   ca ca ca

Ce Ce Ce   ce ce ce

Ci Ci Ci   ci ci ci

Co Co Co   co co co

Cu Cu Cu   cu cu cu

알파벳 D와 d를 써보세요.

D d

D   d

$D\ D\ D$

$d\ d\ d$

$D\ D$

$d\ d$

$D\ D$

$d\ d$

모음과 이어 써보세요.

$Da\ Da\ Da$ $da\ da\ da$

$De\ De\ De$ $de\ de\ de$

$Di\ Di\ Di$ $di\ di\ di$

$Do\ Do\ Do$ $do\ do\ do$

$Du\ Du\ Du$ $du\ du\ du$

Alphabet - Ee

알파벳 E와 e를 써보세요.

	E E E
E e	e e e

E E

e e

E E

e e

모음과 이어 써보세요.

Ea Ea Ea   ea ea ea

Ee Ee Ee   ee ee ee

Ei Ei Ei   ei ei ei

Eo Eo Eo   eo eo eo

Eu Eu Eu   eu eu eu

알파벳 F와 f를 써보세요.

F f

F   f

$\mathcal{F}$ $\mathcal{F}$ $\mathcal{F}$

f f f

$\mathcal{F}$ $\mathcal{F}$

f f

$\mathcal{F}$ $\mathcal{F}$

f f

모음과 이어 써보세요.

Fa Fa Fa   fa fa fa

Fe Fe Fe   fe fe fe

Fi Fi Fi   fi fi fi

Fo Fo Fo   fo fo fo

Fu Fu Fu   fu fu fu

Alphabet - G g

알파벳 G와 g를 써보세요.

G G G

g g g

G G

g g

G G

g g

모음과 이어 써보세요.

Ga Ga Ga   ga ga ga

Ge Ge Ge   ge ge ge

Gi Gi Gi   gi gi gi

Go Go Go   go go go

Gu Gu Gu   gu gu gu

알파벳 H와 h를 써보세요.

H h

H   h

$\mathcal{H}\mathcal{H}\mathcal{H}$

$h\ h\ h$

$\mathcal{H}\mathcal{H}$

$h\ h$

$\mathcal{H}\mathcal{H}$

$h\ h$

모음과 이어 써보세요.

Ha Ha Ha   ha ha ha

He He He   he he he

Hi Hi Hi   hi hi hi

Ho Ho Ho   ho ho ho

Hu Hu Hu   hu hu hu

Alphabet - Ii

알파벳 I와 i를 써보세요.

l l l

i i i

l l

i i

l l

i i

모음과 이어 써보세요. 소문자 i의 점(·)은 이어 쓴 다음, 마지막에 완성하세요.

la la la	ia ia ia
le le le	ie ie ie
li li li	ii ii ii
lo lo lo	io io io
lu lu lu	iu iu iu

알파벳 J와 j를 써보세요.

$\mathcal{J}$ j

J　j

$\mathcal{J}$ $\mathcal{J}$ $\mathcal{J}$

j j j

$\mathcal{J}$ $\mathcal{J}$

j j

$\mathcal{J}$ $\mathcal{J}$

j j

모음과 이어 써보세요. 소문자 j의 점(·)은 이어 쓴 다음, 마지막에 완성하세요.

$\mathcal{J}a$ $\mathcal{J}a$ $\mathcal{J}a$　　　ja ja ja

$\mathcal{J}e$ $\mathcal{J}e$ $\mathcal{J}e$　　　je je je

$\mathcal{J}i$ $\mathcal{J}i$ $\mathcal{J}i$　　　ji ji ji

$\mathcal{J}o$ $\mathcal{J}o$ $\mathcal{J}o$　　　jo jo jo

$\mathcal{J}u$ $\mathcal{J}u$ $\mathcal{J}u$　　　ju ju ju

Alphabet - Kk

알파벳 K와 k를 써보세요.

K k

K K K

k k k

K K

k k

K K

k k

모음과 이어 써보세요.

Ka Ka Ka   ka ka ka

Ke Ke Ke   ke ke ke

Ki Ki Ki   ki ki ki

Ko Ko Ko   ko ko ko

Ku Ku Ku   ku ku ku

알파벳 L과 l을 써보세요.

$\mathcal{L}$ l

$\mathcal{L}$ $\mathcal{L}$ $\mathcal{L}$

l l l

L   l

$\mathcal{L}$ $\mathcal{L}$

l l

$\mathcal{L}$ $\mathcal{L}$

l l

모음과 이어 써보세요.

$\mathcal{L}a$ $\mathcal{L}a$ $\mathcal{L}a$ la la la

$\mathcal{L}e$ $\mathcal{L}e$ $\mathcal{L}e$ le le le

$\mathcal{L}i$ $\mathcal{L}i$ $\mathcal{L}i$ li li li

$\mathcal{L}o$ $\mathcal{L}o$ $\mathcal{L}o$ lo lo lo

$\mathcal{L}u$ $\mathcal{L}u$ $\mathcal{L}u$ lu lu lu

Alphabet - Mm

알파벳 M과 m을 써보세요.

M m

$\mathcal{M}$ m m m

m m m

$\mathcal{M}$ $\mathcal{M}$

m m

$\mathcal{M}$ $\mathcal{M}$

m m

모음과 이어 써보세요.

Ma Ma Ma   ma ma ma

Me Me Me   me me me

Mi Mi Mi   mi mi mi

Mo Mo Mo   mo mo mo

Mu Mu Mu   mu mu mu

알파벳 N과 n을 써보세요.

N n

N   n

n n n

n n n

n n

n n

n n

n n

모음과 이어 써보세요.

Na Na Na　　　　*na na na*

Ne Ne Ne　　　　*ne ne ne*

Ni Ni Ni　　　　*ni ni ni*

No No No　　　　*no no no*

Nu Nu Nu　　　　*nu nu nu*

Practice Note

DAY 2

알파벳 Oo부터 Zz까지
연습하는 날

Alphabet - Oo

알파벳 O와 o를 써보세요.

O O O

O O O

O O

O O

O O

O O

모음과 이어 써보세요.

Oa Oa Oa   oa oa oa

Oe Oe Oe   oe oe oe

Oi Oi Oi   oi oi oi

Oo Oo Oo   oo oo oo

Ou Ou Ou   ou ou ou

알파벳 P와 p를 써보세요.

P   p

p p
p p
p p
p p

모음과 이어 써보세요.

Pa Pa Pa   pa pa pa

Pe Pe Pe   pe pe pe

Pi Pi Pi   pi pi pi

Po Po Po   po po po

Pu Pu Pu   pu pu pu

Alphabet - 2q

알파벳 Q와 q를 써보세요.

Q   q

2 2 2

q q q

2 2

q q

2 2

q q

모음과 이어 써보세요.

Qa Qa Qa	qa qa qa
Qe Qe Qe	qe qe qe
Qi Qi Qi	qi qi qi
Qo Qo Qo	qo qo qo
Qu Qu Qu	qu qu qu

알파벳 R과 r을 써보세요.

R R R

ƨ ƨ ƨ

R   r

R R

ƨ ƨ

R R

ƨ ƨ

모음과 이어 써보세요.

Ra Ra Ra   ra ra ra

Re Re Re   re re re

Ri Ri Ri   ri ri ri

Ro Ro Ro   ro ro ro

Ru Ru Ru   ru ru ru

Alphabet - Ss

알파벳 S와 s를 써보세요.

S　s

모음과 이어 써보세요.

Sa Sa Sa   sa sa sa

Se Se Se   se se se

Si Si Si   si si si

So So So   so so so

Su Su Su   su su su

알파벳 T와 t를 써보세요.

T T T

t t t

T

t t

T

t t

모음과 이어 써보세요. 소문자 t의 선(-)은 이어 쓴 다음, 마지막에 완성하세요.

Ta Ta Ta   ta ta ta

Te Te Te   te te te

Ti Ti Ti   ti ti ti

To To To   to to to

Tu Tu Tu   tu tu tu

알파벳 U와 u를 써보세요.

$\mathcal{U}$ u

U   u

U U U

u u u

U U

u u

U U

u u

모음과 이어 써보세요.

Ua Ua Ua   ua ua ua

Ue Ue Ue   ue ue ue

Ui Ui Ui   ui ui ui

Uo Uo Uo   uo uo uo

Uu Uu Uu   uu uu uu

알파벳 V와 v를 써보세요.

$\mathcal{V}$ $\mathcal{V}$ $\mathcal{V}$

v v v

V   v

$\mathcal{V}$ $\mathcal{V}$

v v

$\mathcal{V}$ $\mathcal{V}$

v v

모음과 이어 써보세요.

$\mathcal{V}a$ $\mathcal{V}a$ $\mathcal{V}a$ va va va

$\mathcal{V}e$ $\mathcal{V}e$ $\mathcal{V}e$ ve ve ve

$\mathcal{V}i$ $\mathcal{V}i$ $\mathcal{V}i$ vi vi vi

$\mathcal{V}o$ $\mathcal{V}o$ $\mathcal{V}o$ vo vo vo

$\mathcal{V}u$ $\mathcal{V}u$ $\mathcal{V}u$ vu vu vu

Alphabet - Ww

알파벳 W와 w를 써보세요.

W w

W   w

W W W

w w w

W W

w w

W W

w w

모음과 이어 써보세요.

Wa Wa Wa   wa wa wa

We We We   we we we

Wi Wi Wi   wi wi wi

Wo Wo Wo   wo wo wo

Wu Wu Wu   wu wu wu

알파벳 X와 x를 써보세요.

X x

X X X

x x x

X X

x x

X X

x x

모음과 이어 써보세요. 소문자 x의 선(/)은 이어 쓴 다음, 마지막에 완성하세요.

Xa Xa Xa   xa xa xa

Xe Xe Xe   xe xe xe

Xi Xi Xi   xi xi xi

Xo Xo Xo   xo xo xo

Xu Xu Xu   xu xu xu

Alphabet - Yy

알파벳 Y와 y를 써보세요.

Y y

Y y

Y Y Y

y y y

Y Y

y y

Y Y

y y

모음과 이어 써보세요.

Ya Ya Ya   ya ya ya

Ye Ye Ye   ye ye ye

Yi Yi Yi   yi yi yi

Yo Yo Yo   yo yo yo

Yu Yu Yu   yu yu yu

알파벳 Z와 z를 써보세요.

Z *z*

Z Z Z

z z z

Z Z

z z

Z Z

z z

모음과 이어 써보세요.

Za Za Za   za za za

Ze Ze Ze   ze ze ze

Zi Zi Zi   zi zi zi

Zo Zo Zo   zo zo zo

Zu Zu Zu   zu zu zu

Alphabet A-Z

알파벳 대문자를 이어 써보세요.

ABCDEFGHIJKLMNOPQRSTUVWXYZ

ABCDEFGHIJKLMNOPQRSTUVWXYZ

ABCDEFGHIJKLMNOPQRSTUVWXYZ

알파벳 소문자를 한 번에 이어 써보세요. i, j, t, x의 점과 선은 마지막에 쓰세요.

abcdefghijklmnopqrstuvwxyz

abcdefghijklmnopqrstuvwxyz

abcdefghijklmnopqrstuvwxyz

Practice Note

DAY 3

Aa부터 Mm까지
다양한 단어를 연습하는 날

DAY 3

Words - Aa

A a

A a

$a\ a\ a$

$a\ a\ a$

알파벳 a가 앞, 중간, 끝에 들어가는 단어를 연습해보세요.

sea
바다

sea sea

habit
습관

habit habit

alphabet
알파벳

alphabet alphabet

treasure
보물

treasure treasure

umbrella
우산

umbrella umbrella

Bb

B b

B b

B B B

b b b

알파벳 b가 앞, 중간, 끝에 들어가는 단어를 연습해보세요.

bear 곰	*bear bear*
climb 오르다	*climb climb*
bubble 거품	*bubble bubble*
symbol 상징	*symbol symbol*
republic 공화국	*republic republic*

47

Words - Cc

C c

C C C

c c c

C   c

알파벳 c가 앞, 중간, 끝에 들어가는 단어를 연습해보세요.

chance

기회

chance chance

source

근원

source source

public

공공의

public public

cursive

필기체인

cursive cursive

respect

존경

respect respect

$\mathcal{D}$ d

D d

D D D

d d d

알파벳 d가 앞, 중간, 끝에 들어가는 단어를 연습해보세요.

dog
개

dog dog

mind
마음

mind mind

dream
꿈

dream dream

parade
가두 행진

parade parade

adventure
모험

adventure adventure

49

Words - Ee

E e

E   e

$\mathcal{E}$ $\mathcal{E}$ $\mathcal{E}$

e e e

알파벳 e가 앞, 중간, 끝에 들어가는 단어를 연습해보세요.

event
사건

event event

couple
두 사람

couple couple

present
현재

present present

strange
이상한

strange strange

together
함께

together together

F f

F F F

f f f

F   f

알파벳 f가 앞, 중간, 끝에 들어가는 단어를 연습해보세요.

cafe
카페

cafe cafe

loaf
덩어리

loaf loaf

chief
상사

chief chief

fruit
과일

fruit fruit

fortunately
운좋게

fortunately fortunately

Words - Gg

G g

G   g

알파벳 g가 앞, 중간, 끝에 들어가는 단어를 연습해보세요.

sign
징후

sign sign

glory
영광

glory glory

spring
봄

spring spring

greeting
인사

greeting greeting

magazine
잡지

magazine magazine

H h

H   h

HHH

h h h

알파벳 h가 앞, 중간, 끝에 들어가는 단어를 연습해보세요.

honor
명예

honor honor

speech
연설

speech speech

delight
기쁨

delight delight

triumph
승리

triumph triumph

neighbor
이웃

neighbor neighbor

Words - Ii

I i

l l l
i i i

I i

알파벳 i가 앞, 중간, 끝에 들어가는 단어를 연습해보세요.

anti
~~~~~
반대하는

anti anti

**idea**
~~~~~
생각

idea idea

invent
~~~~~
발명하다

invent invent

**similar**
~~~~~
비슷한

similar similar

various
~~~~~
여러 가지의

various various

J   j

알파벳 j가 앞, 중간, 끝에 들어가는 단어를 연습해보세요.

joy
기쁨

joy joy

judge
재판관

judge judge

juice
주스

juice juice

Beijing
베이징

Beijing Beijing

journey
여행

journey journey

Words - Kk

K K K

k k k

K k

알파벳 k가 앞, 중간, 끝에 들어가는 단어를 연습해보세요.

sky
하늘

sky sky

dark
어두운

dark dark

kind
친절한

kind kind

like
좋아하다

like like

luck
행운

luck luck

$\mathcal{L}\ \mathcal{L}\ \mathcal{L}$

$\ell\ \ell\ \ell$

L l

알파벳 l이 앞, 중간, 끝에 들어가는 단어를 연습해보세요.

cool
시원한

cool cool

feel
느끼다

feel feel

light
빛

light light

language
언어

language language

celebrate
축하하다

celebrate celebrate

Words - Mm

M m
M   m

알파벳 m이 앞, 중간, 끝에 들어가는 단어를 연습해보세요.

calm
평온한

calm calm

farm
농장

farm farm

memory
기억

memory memory

amazing
놀라운

amazing amazing

mystery
신비

mystery mystery

Practice Note

Practice Note

DAY 4

Nn부터 Zz까지
다양한 단어를 연습하는 날

Words - Nn

$\mathcal{N}$ n

N   n

n n n

n n n

알파벳 n이 앞, 중간, 끝에 들어가는 단어를 연습해보세요.

bean
콩

bean bean

noble
고귀한

noble noble

shine
빛나다

shine shine

candle
양초

candle candle

design
디자인

design design

$\mathcal{O}\ \mathcal{o}$

$\mathcal{O}$

O o

$\mathcal{O}\ \mathcal{O}\ \mathcal{O}$

$\mathcal{o}\ \mathcal{o}\ \mathcal{o}$

알파벳 o가 앞, 중간, 끝에 들어가는 단어를 연습해보세요.

owl
부엉이

$owl\ owl$

open
열다

$open\ open$

voice
목소리

$voice\ voice$

potato
감자

$potato\ potato$

favorite
아주 좋아하는

$favorite\ favorite$

P p

P p

p p p

p p p

알파벳 p가 앞, 중간, 끝에 들어가는 단어를 연습해보세요.

pray
빌다

pray pray

cheap
값싼

cheap cheap

practice
연습

practice practice

support
지지하다

support support

appointment
약속

appointment appointment

Q q

$\mathcal{Q}$ $\mathcal{Q}$ $\mathcal{Q}$

q q q

알파벳 q가 앞, 중간, 끝에 들어가는 단어를 연습해보세요.

Iraq
이라크

Iraq Iraq

equal
같은, 동등한

equal equal

quiet
조용한

quiet quiet

square
정사각형

square square

question
질문

question question

Words - Rr

R r

R   r

알파벳 r이 앞, 중간, 끝에 들어가는 단어를 연습해보세요.

color
색

color color

marry
결혼하다

marry marry

regular
규칙적인

regular regular

graduate
졸업하다

graduate graduate

photographer
사진사

photographer photographer

$\mathcal{S}\ \mathcal{S}\ \mathcal{S}$

$\mathit{s}\ \mathit{s}\ \mathit{s}$

S   s

알파벳 s가 앞, 중간, 끝에 들어가는 단어를 연습해보세요.

pass 지나가다	*pass pass*
trust 신뢰	*trust trust*
shake 흔들다	*shake shake*
summer 여름	*summer summer*
whisper 속삭이다	*whisper whisper*

Words - Tt

T T T

t t t

T   t

알파벳 t가 앞, 중간, 끝에 들어가는 단어를 연습해보세요.

art
예술

art art

poet
시인

poet poet

winter
겨울

winter winter

autumn
가을

autumn autumn

tradition
전통

tradition tradition

$\mathcal{U}$ u

U u

$\mathcal{U}$ $\mathcal{U}$ $\mathcal{U}$

u u u

알파벳 u가 앞, 중간, 끝에 들어가는 단어를 연습해보세요.

flu
감기

flu flu

adult
성인

adult adult

unity
일치

unity unity

dialogue
대화

dialogue dialogue

universe
우주

universe universe

Words - Vo

$\mathcal{V}$ v

V   v

V V V

v v v

알파벳 v가 앞, 중간, 끝에 들어가는 단어를 연습해보세요.

TV
텔레비전

TV TV

advice
충고

advice advice

heaven
천국

heaven heaven

voyage
항해

voyage voyage

vacation
휴가

vacation vacation

W w

W   w

W W W

w w w

알파벳 w가 앞, 중간, 끝에 들어가는 단어를 연습해보세요.

| know | *know know* |
| 알다 | |

| view | *view view* |
| 경치 | |

| jewel | *jewel jewel* |
| 보석 | |

| world | *world world* |
| 세계 | |

| worth | *worth worth* |
| 가치 | |

Words - Xx

X x

X X X

x x x

X   x

알파벳 x가 앞, 중간, 끝에 들어가는 단어를 연습해보세요.

box
상자

box box

relax
편안해지다

relax relax

explore
탐험하다

explore explore

excellent
훌륭한

excellent excellent

xylophone
실로폰

xylophone xylophone

Yy

Y y

Y Y Y

y y y

알파벳 y가 앞, 중간, 끝에 들어가는 단어를 연습해보세요.

today
오늘

today today

beauty
아름다움

beauty beauty

yellow
노란색

yellow yellow

liberty
자유

liberty liberty

yesterday
어제

yesterday yesterday

Words - Zz

Z   z

Z Z Z

Z Z Z

알파벳 z가 앞, 중간, 끝에 들어가는 단어를 연습해보세요.

zoo
동물원

zoo zoo

jazz
재즈

jazz jazz

quiz
퀴즈

quiz quiz

pizza
피자

pizza pizza

puzzle
수수께끼

puzzle puzzle

Practice Note

Practice Note

DAY 5

주제별 단어를 연습하는 날
숫자, 월, 요일, 그리스 신, 태양계, 식물

DAY

5

 Numbers

숫자를 영어 필기체로 써보세요.

one
~~~
1

*one one*

**two**
~~~
2

two two

three
~~~
3

*three three*

**four**
~~~
4

four four

five
~~~
5

*five five*

**six**
~~~
6

six six

seven
7

seven seven

eight
8

eight eight

nine
9

nine nine

ten
10

ten ten

hundred
100

hundred hundred

thousand
1000

thousand thousand

Months of the Year

열두 달을 영어 필기체로 써보세요.

January
1월

January January

February
2월

February February

March
3월

March March

April
4월

April April

May
5월

May May

June
6월

June June

July	*July July*
7월	

August	*August August*
8월	

September	*September September*
9월	

October	*October October*
10월	

November	*November November*
11월	

December	*December December*
12월	

Days of the Week

요일을 영어 필기체로 써보세요.

Monday
~~~
월요일

*Monday Monday*

**Tuesday**
~~~
화요일

Tuesday Tuesday

Wednesday
~~~
수요일

*Wednesday Wednesday*

**Thursday**
~~~
목요일

Thursday Thursday

Friday
~~~
금요일

*Friday Friday*

**Saturday**
~~~
토요일

Saturday Saturday

Sunday	Sunday Sunday
일요일	

date	date date
날짜	

day	day day
날	

week	week week
주	

month	month month
월	

year	year year
해	

The Gods

그리스 신화 속 12신의 이름을 영어 필기체로 써보세요.

Zeus

제우스
제왕의 신

Zeus Zeus

Hera

헤라
출산의 여신

Hera Hera

Poseidon

포세이돈
바다의 신

Poseidon Poseidon

Demeter

데메테르
대지의 여신

Demeter Demeter

Athena

아테나
지혜의 여신

Athena Athena

Apollon

아폴론
의술의 신

Apollon Apollon

in Greek Mythology

Artemis

아르테미스
사냥의 여신

Artemis Artemis

Ares

아레스
전쟁의 신

Ares Ares

Aphrodite

아프로디테
사랑의 여신

Aphrodite Aphrodite

Hermes

헤르메스
상업의 신

Hermes Hermes

Hephaestus

헤파이스토스
불의 신

Hephaestus Hephaestus

Dionysus

디오니소스
술의 신

Dionysus Dionysus

Solar System

태양계에 있는 것들의 이름을 영어 필기체로 써보세요.

Sun
태양

Sun Sun

Moon
달

Moon Moon

Mercury
수성

Mercury Mercury

Venus
금성

Venus Venus

Earth
지구

Earth Earth

Mars
화성

Mars Mars

Jupiter
목성

Jupiter Jupiter

Saturn
토성

Saturn Saturn

Uranus
천왕성

Uranus Uranus

Neptune
해왕성

Neptune Neptune

Pluto
명왕성

Pluto Pluto

planet
행성

planet planet

DAY

5

식물의 이름을 영어 필기체로 써보세요.

rose
장미

rose rose

lily
백합

lily lily

ivy
아이비
(담쟁이덩굴)

ivy ivy

bamboo
대나무

bamboo bamboo

pine tree
소나무

pine tree pine tree

dahlia
달리아

dahlia dahlia

freesia

프리지어

freesia freesia

cosmos

코스모스

cosmos cosmos

monstera

몬스테라

monstera monstera

camellia

동백나무

camellia camellia

gypsophila

안개꽃

gypsophila gypsophila

hydrangea

수국

hydrangea hydrangea

Practice Note

Practice Note

DAY 6

일상에 유용한 단어를 연습하는 날
한국인 성, 유명인 이름, 수도와 나라

Korean Last Names

한국인의 성을 영어 필기체로 써보세요.

Kim
김

Kim Kim

Lee
이

Lee Lee

Park
박

Park Park

Choi
최

Choi Choi

Jung
정

Jung Jung

Kang
강

Kang Kang

Cho
조

Cho Cho

Jang
장

Jang Jang

Lim
임

Lim Lim

Han
한

Han Han

Seo
서

Seo Seo

Shin
신

Shin Shin

Korean Last Names

한국인의 성을 영어 필기체로 써보세요.

Kwon
권

Kwon Kwon

Hwang
황

Hwang Hwang

Ahn
안

Ahn Ahn

Song
송

Song Song

Ryu
류

Ryu Ryu

Jeon
전

Jeon Jeon

Hong

홍

Hong Hong

Heo

허

Heo Heo

Yang

양

Yang Yang

Son

손

Son Son

Bae

배

Bae Bae

Oh

오

Oh Oh

유명인의 이름을 영어 필기체로 써보세요.

Steve Jobs
스티브 잡스

Steve Jobs   Steve Jobs

Oprah Winfrey
오프라 윈프리

Oprah Winfrey   Oprah Winfrey

Warren Buffett
워렌 버핏

Warren Buffett   Warren Buffett

Yuna Kim
김연아

Yuna Kim   Yuna Kim

Hyunjin Ryu
류현진

Hyunjin Ryu   Hyunjin Ryu

Heungmin Son
손흥민

Heungmin Son   Heungmin Son

Famous People

Albert Camus
알베르 카뮈

Albert Camus   Albert Camus

Michael Jordan
마이클 조던

Michael Jordan   Michael Jordan

Martin Scorsese
마틴 스코세이지

Martin Scorsese   Martin Scorsese

Clint Eastwood
클린트 이스트우드

Clint Eastwood   Clint Eastwood

Abraham Lincoln
에이브러햄 링컨

Abraham Lincoln   Abraham Lincoln

Ernest Hemingway
어니스트 헤밍웨이

Ernest Hemingway   Ernest Hemingway

Names of

유명인의 이름을 영어 필기체로 써보세요.

Friedrich Nietzsche
프리드리히 니체

Friedrich Nietzsche Friedrich Nietzsche

Ludwig van Beethoven
루트비히 판 베토벤

Ludwig van Beethoven
Ludwig van Beethoven

William Shakespeare
윌리엄 셰익스피어

William Shakespeare
William Shakespeare

Johann Sebastian Bach
요한 제바스티안 바흐

Johann Sebastian Bach
Johann Sebastian Bach

Hermann Hesse
헤르만 헤세

Hermann Hesse Hermann Hesse

Virginia Woolf
버지니아 울프

Virginia Woolf Virginia Woolf

Famous People

Lucy Maud Montgomery

루시 모드 몽고메리

Lucy Maud Montgomery

Lucy Maud Montgomery

Lewis Carroll

루이스 캐럴

Lewis Carroll   Lewis Carroll

Albert Einstein

알베르트 아인슈타인

Albert Einstein   Albert Einstein

Isaac Newton

아이작 뉴턴

Isaac Newton   Isaac Newton

Elon Musk

일론 머스크

Elon Musk   Elon Musk

Leonardo DiCaprio

리어나도 디캐프리오

Leonardo DiCaprio   Leonardo DiCaprio

Capital Cities

수도와 나라 이름을 영어 필기체로 써보세요.

Vienna
비엔나(빈)
Austria
오스트리아

Vienna Vienna

Austria Austria

Brussels
브뤼셀
Belgium
벨기에

Brussels Brussels

Belgium Belgium

Ottawa
오타와
Canada
캐나다

Ottawa Ottawa

Canada Canada

Copenhagen
코펜하겐
Denmark
덴마크

Copenhagen Copenhagen

Denmark Denmark

Quito
키토
Ecuador
에콰도르

Quito Quito

Ecuador Ecuador

Paris
파리
France
프랑스

Paris Paris

France France

and Countries

Athens 아테네 **Greece** 그리스	*Athens Athens* *Greece Greece*
Budapest 부다페스트 **Hungary** 헝가리	*Budapest Budapest* *Hungary Hungary*
Rome 로마 **Italy** 이탈리아	*Rome Rome* *Italy Italy*
Tokyo 도쿄 **Japan** 일본	*Tokyo Tokyo* *Japan Japan*
Nairobi 나이로비 **Kenya** 케냐	*Nairobi Nairobi* *Kenya Kenya*
Beirut 베이루트 **Lebanon** 레바논	*Beirut Beirut* *Lebanon Lebanon*

Capital Cities

수도와 나라 이름을 영어 필기체로 써보세요.

Rabat
라바트
Morocco
모로코

Rabat Rabat

Morocco Morocco

Amsterdam
암스테르담
Netherlands
네덜란드

Amsterdam Amsterdam

Netherlands Netherlands

Muscat
무스카트
Oman
오만

Muscat Muscat

Oman Oman

Lisbon
리스본
Portugal
포르투갈

Lisbon Lisbon

Portugal Portugal

Doha
도하
Qatar
카타르

Doha Doha

Qatar Qatar

Moscow
모스크바
Russia
러시아

Moscow Moscow

Russia Russia

and Countries

Bern 베른 **Switzerland** 스위스	Bern Bern Switzerland Switzerland
Ankara 앙카라 **Turkiye** 튀르키예	Ankara Ankara Turkiye Turkiye
Montevideo 몬테비데오 **Uruguay** 우루과이	Montevideo Montevideo Uruguay Uruguay
Caracas 카라카스 **Venezuela** 베네수엘라	Caracas Caracas Venezuela Venezuela
Lusaka 루사카 **Zambia** 잠비아	Lusaka Lusaka Zambia Zambia
Sanaa 사나 **Yemen** 예멘	Sanaa Sanaa Yemen Yemen

Practice Note

Practice Note

DAY 7

문장에 자주 활용되는 단어를
연습하는 날

Commonly

문장에 자주 활용되는 단어를 연습해보세요.

| I i 나는 | I I |
| | i i |

| You you 당신은 | You You |
| | you you |

| He he 그는 | He He |
| | he he |

| She she 그녀는 | She She |
| | she she |

| They they 그들은 | They They |
| | they they |

| We we 우리는 | We We |
| | we we |

Used Words

My **my** 〰 나의	*My My*
	my my
Your **your** 〰 당신의	*Your Your*
	your your
His **his** 〰 그의	*His His*
	his his
Her **her** 〰 그녀의	*Her Her*
	her her
Their **their** 〰 그들의	*Their Their*
	their their
Our **our** 〰 우리들의	*Our Our*
	our our

Commonly

문장에 자주 활용되는 단어를 연습해보세요.

| This this 이것 | This This |
| | this this |

| That that 저것 | That That |
| | that that |

| It it 그것 | It It |
| | it it |

| What what 무엇 | What What |
| | what what |

| Who who 누구 | Who Who |
| | who who |

| Whose whose 누구의 | Whose Whose |
| | whose whose |

Used Words

When **when** 언제	*When When* *when when*
Where **where** 어디서	*Where Where* *where where*
Why **why** 왜	*Why Why* *why why*
Which **which** 어느	*Which Which* *which which*
How **how** 어떻게	*How How* *how how*
While **while** 동안에	*While While* *while while*

문장에 자주 활용되는 단어를 연습해보세요.

Will **will** ~일 것이다	*Will Will* *will will*
Would **would** will의 과거	*Would Would* *would would*
Shall **shall** ~할 것이다	*Shall Shall* *shall shall*
Should **should** ~해야 한다	*Should Should* *should should*
Can **can** ~ 할 수 있다	*Can Can* *can can*
Could **could** can의 과거	*Could Could* *could could*

Used Words

After after 뒤에	After After
	after after

And and 그리고	And And
	and and

As as 하는 동안에	As As
	as as

Because because 때문에	Because Because
	because because

Between between 사이에	between between
	between between

But but 그러나	But But
	but but

문장에 자주 활용되는 단어를 연습해보세요.

| **To** **to** ~로 | To To |
| | to to |

| **For** **for** 위해서 | For For |
| | for for |

| **From** **from** ~로부터 | From From |
| | from from |

| **However** **however** 그러나 | However However |
| | however however |

| **If** **if** 만약 ~라면 | If If |
| | if if |

| **Or** **or** 또는 | Or Or |
| | or or |

Used Words

Since **since** 이후에	Since Since since since
So **so** 그래서	So So so so
The **the** 그	The The the the
Then **then** 그때는	Then Then then then
Up **up** 위로	Up Up up up
Down **down** 아래로	Down Down down down

Practice Note

DAY 8

일상에 유용한 문장을 연습하는 날
일상, 응원·위로의 말, 긍정 확언, 명언

Common Expressions

일상에서 자주 쓰는 표현을 영어 필기체로 써보세요.

Congratulations!
축하해요.

Congratulations!

I love you.
사랑해요.

I love you.

That's a good idea.
좋은 생각이에요.

That's a good idea.

Thank you very much.
정말 고맙습니다.

Thank you very much.

Have a good day!

좋은 하루 보내세요.

Have a good day!

I wish you the best of luck.

행운을 빌어요.

I wish you the best of luck.

I hope everything is okay.

별일 없었으면 좋겠어요.

I hope everything is okay.

All the best wishes for you!

당신에게 모든 행운이 깃들기를 바랍니다!

All the best wishes for you!

Words of

응원과 위로의 말을 영어 필기체로 써보세요.

You're doing great.

당신은 잘하고 있어요.

You're doing great.

I'm sure you can do it.

당신은 할 수 있어요.

I'm sure you can do it.

I wish you success.

좋은 결과가 있기를 바랄게요.

I wish you success.

Think on the bright side.

긍정적으로 생각하세요.

Think on the bright side.

Encouragement

Don't worry about it.

걱정하지 마세요.

Don't worry about it.

Stay strong and get well soon.

힘내시고 빨리 회복하세요.

Stay strong and get well soon.

I hope you feel better soon.

건강이 좋아지기를 바랍니다.

I hope you feel better soon.

I am so sorry to hear about your loss.

삼가 조의를 표합니다.

I am so sorry to hear about your loss.

 Positive Affirmation

나를 위한 긍정 확언을 영어 필기체로 써보세요.

I believe in myself.

나는 나 자신을 믿는다.

I believe in myself.

I've got this!

나는 할 수 있다.

I've got this!

I will keep going.

나는 계속 할거다.

I will keep going.

I love myself for who I am.

나는 있는 그대로의 나를 사랑한다.

I love myself for who I am.

I am grateful for all the blessings.

나는 모든 축복에 감사한다.

I am grateful for all the blessings.

Today is going to be a great day.

오늘은 좋은 날이 될 것이다.

Today is going to be a great day.

I can do anything but not everything.

나는 모든 것을 다 할 수는 없지만 어떤 것도 할 수 있다.

I can do anything but not everything.

Believing in myself is the first secret to success.

나 자신을 믿는 것이 성공하는 첫 번째 열쇠다.

Believing in myself is the first secret to success.

Famous Quotes

지혜를 주는 명언을 영어 필기체로 써보세요.

No pain, no gain.

고통 없이는, 얻는 것도 없다.

No pain, no gain.

This too shall pass away.

이 또한 지나갈 것이다.

This too shall pass away.

Never let your fear decide your future.

두려움이 미래를 결정하게 하지 말라.

Never let your fear decide your future.

If you change nothing, nothing will change.

아무것도 바꾸지 않으면 아무것도 변하지 않는다.

If you change nothing, nothing will change.

Happiness can exist only in acceptance.

행복은 오직 내가 받아들이려고 할 때 존재한다. (조지 오웰)

Happiness can exist only in acceptance.

Everything you can imagine is real.

당신이 상상하는 모든 것이 현실이 된다. (파블로 피카소)

Everything you can imagine is real.

Life itself is the most wonderful fairy tale.

인생이야말로 가장 아름다운 동화다. (한스 크리스티안 안데르센)

Life itself is the most wonderful fairy tale.

Attitude is a little thing that makes a big difference.

태도는 아주 사소하지만 큰 차이를 만든다. (윈스턴 처칠)

Attitude is a little thing that makes a big difference.

Practice Note

Practice Note

DAY 9

특별한 날에 사용되는 문구를 연습하는 날
크리스마스, 새해, 생일, 기념의 말

Season's Greetings

크리스마스와 새해 인사를 영어 필기체로 써보세요.

We wish you a Merry Christmas!
즐거운 크리스마스가 되시길 바랍니다.

We wish you a Merry Christmas!

Season's greetings to all of you.
즐거운 크리스마스와 행복한 새해 되세요.

Season's greetings to all of you.

May God bless your home with peace, joy and love.
신이 여러분에게 평화와 기쁨, 사랑의 축복을 내리시기를 빕니다.

May God bless your home with peace, joy and love.

Wishing you a day full of happiness this Christmas.
이번 크리스마스에 행복 가득하기를 빕니다.

Wishing you a day full of happiness this Christmas.

Happy New Year!

행복한 새해가 되세요.

Happy New Year!

Best wishes for the New Year.

새해 복 많이 받으세요.

Best wishes for the New Year.

We hope this year to be best year ever.

최고의 한 해가 되길 바랍니다.

We hope this year to be best year ever.

I wish that all your wishes are fulfilled this year.

새해에는 모든 소망들이 이루어지길 바랍니다.

I wish that all your wishes are fulfilled this year.

생일 축하 인사와 축복의 말을 영어 필기체로 써보세요.

Happy Birthday to you!

생일 축하합니다!

Happy Birthday to you!

Wish you all the happiness in the world.

당신에게 세상의 모든 행복이 있기를.

Wish you all the happiness in the world.

May joy, love and laughter be with you!

기쁨, 사랑, 웃음이 함께하기를!

May joy, love and laughter be with you!

May all your dreams come true!

당신의 꿈이 모두 이루어지기를!

May all your dreams come true!

밸런타인데이 인사를 영어 필기체로 써보세요.

Happy Valentine's Day!

행복한 밸런타인데이 보내세요.

Happy Valentine's Day!

I love you with all my heart.

당신을 진심으로 사랑합니다.

I love you with all my heart.

You're always on my mind and in my heart.

당신은 항상 제 생각과 마음속에 있습니다.

You're always on my mind and in my heart.

You've made my life complete!

당신이 제 삶을 완전하게 만들어줬어요.

You've made my life complete!

For Parent's Day

어버이날 인사를 영어 필기체로 써보세요.

Happy Parents' Day!

행복한 어버이날 되세요!

Happy Parents' Day!

Wishing you a very special Parents' Day!

특별한 어버이날 보내세요.

Wishing you a very special Parents' Day!

Because of you, I am who I am.

당신이 있기에, 제가 있습니다.

Because of you, I am who I am.

Thank you for always being there for me.

늘 곁에 있어주셔서 감사해요.

Thank you for always being there for me.

Thank you for being my mom & dad.

저의 어머니, 아버지가 되어주셔서 감사합니다.

Thank you for being my mom & dad.

You're in all my favorite memories.

저의 가장 소중한 기억 속에 당신이 계십니다.

You're in all my favorite memories.

Thinking of you with love today and always.

오늘뿐만 아니라 항상 당신을 사랑하고 있습니다.

Thinking of you with love today and always.

Thank you for always taking such great care of me.

항상 보살펴주셔서 감사해요.

Thank you for always taking such great care of me.

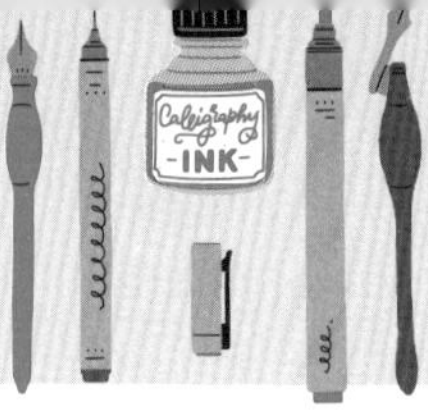

Practice Note

Practice Note

DAY 10

세계 문학 작품의 제목과 문단을 연습하는 날
오만과 편견, 노인과 바다, 어린 왕자

세계 문학 작품의 제목을 영어 필기체로 써보세요.

Demian

데미안(1919, 헤르만 헤세)

Demian

East of Eden

에덴의 동쪽(1952, 존 스타인벡)

East of Eden

Animal Farm

동물농장(1945, 조지 오웰)

Animal Farm

The Last Leaf

마지막 잎새(1905, 오 헨리)

The Last Leaf

Literature Books

Great Expectations

위대한 유산(1861, 찰스 디킨스)

Great Expectations

Lord of the Flies

파리대왕(1954, 윌리엄 골딩)

Lord of the Flies

The Great Gatsby

위대한 개츠비(1925, 프랜시스 스콧 피츠제럴드)

The Great Gatsby

Pride and Prejudice

오만과 편견(1813, 제인 오스틴)

Pride and Prejudice

Classic English

세계 문학 작품의 제목을 영어 필기체로 써보세요.

The Old Man and the Sea

노인과 바다(1952, 어니스트 헤밍웨이)

The Old Man and the Sea

The Moon and Sixpence

달과 6펜스(1919년, 윌리엄 서머싯 몸)

The Moon and Sixpence

A Farewell to Arms

무기여 잘 있거라(1929, 어니스트 헤밍웨이)

A Farewell to Arms

The Catcher in the Rye

호밀밭의 파수꾼(1951, 제롬 데이비드 샐린저)

The Catcher in the Rye

Literature Books

Alice's Adventures in Wonderland

이상한 나라의 앨리스(1865, 루이스 캐럴)

Alice's Adventures in Wonderland

The Merchant of Venice

베니스의 상인(1596~1598, 윌리엄 셰익스피어)

The Merchant of Venice

The Adventures of Tom Sawyer

톰 소여의 모험(1876, 마크 트웨인)

The Adventures of Tom Sawyer

A Streetcar Named Desire

욕망이라는 이름의 전차(1947, 테네시 윌리엄스)

A Streetcar Named Desire

세계 문학 작품 속 한 문단을 영어 필기체로 써보세요.

Pride and Prejudice
By Jane Austen

오만과 편견 제인 오스틴

"But vanity, not love, has been my folly.
Pleased with the preference of one,
and offended by the neglect of the other,
on the very beginning of our acquaintance,
I have courted prepossession and ignorance,
and driven reason away,
where either were concerned.
Till this moment I never knew myself."

"그렇지만 그건 사랑이 아니라 어리석은 허영심이었어.
처음 만났을 때 한 사람은 나를 무시해서 기분이 언짢았고,
다른 한 사람은 특별한 호감을 표시해서 기분이 좋았어.
이성적인 판단 없이 선입견과 무지로 두 사람을 대했던 거야.
지금 이 순간까지 난, 나 자신에 대해 모르고 있었지."

Literature Books

"But vanity, not love, has been my folly.

Pleased with the preference of one,

and offended by the neglect of the other,

on the very beginning of our acquaintance,

I have courted prepossession and ignorance,

and driven reason away,

where either were concerned.

Till this moment I never knew myself."

세계 문학 작품 속 한 문단을 영어 필기체로 써보세요.

The Old Man and the Sea
By Ernest Hemingway

노인과 바다 어니스트 헤밍웨이

He settled comfortably against the wood
and took his suffering as it came
and the fish swam steadily
and the boat moved slowly through the dark water.
There was a small sea rising with the wind
coming up from the east and at noon
the old man's left hand was uncramped.

노인은 편안하게 뱃전에 몸을 기댄 채 들이닥치는 고통을 견뎌냈다.
물고기는 조금도 흐트러지지 않는 모습으로 헤엄쳐 나갔고,
배는 검은 물살을 헤치며 천천히 움직였다.
동쪽에서 바람이 불어오기 시작하자 파도가 조금 일었고,
정오가 되어서야 비로소 노인의 왼손에 난 경련이 사그라들었다.

Literature Books

He settled comfortably against the wood
and took his suffering as it came
and the fish swam steadily
and the boat moved slowly through the dark water.
There was a small sea rising with the wind
coming up from the east and at noon
the old man's left hand was uncramped.

세계 문학 작품 속 한 문단을 영어 필기체로 써보세요.

The Little Prince
By Antoine de Saint-Exupéry

어린 왕자 앙투안 드 생텍쥐페리

"If, for example,
you come at four o'clock in the afternoon,
then at three o'clock I shall begin to be happy.
I shall feel happier and happier as the hour advances.
At four o'clock, I shall already be worrying
and jumping about.
I shall show you how happy I am!"

"만약 네가 오후 4시에 온다면
나는 3시부터 행복해지기 시작할 거야.
시간이 갈수록 난 점점 더 행복해지겠지.
4시에는 흥분해서 안절부절못할 거야.
그래서 행복이 얼마나 값진 것인지 알게 되겠지."

Literature Books

"If, for example,

you come at four o'clock in the afternoon,

then at three o'clock I shall begin to be happy.

I shall feel happier and happier as the hour advances.

At four o'clock, I shall already be worrying

and jumping about.

I shall show you how happy I am!"

Practice Note

Practice Note

Certificate
of Completion

10 days of English Cursive Handwriting Workbook

Congratulations!

Name _____

Date of Birth _____

Address _____

The date of Completion _____

Signature _____